It Happened to

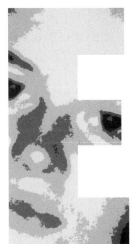

ME

Teenage Pregnancy

Interviews by Suzie Hayman and Helen Elliott

Photography by Laurence Cendrowicz

W
FRANKLIN WATTS
LONDON SYDNEY

This edition 2005

Franklin Watts
96 Leonard Street
London
EC2A 4XD

Franklin Watts Australia
Level 17/207 Kent Street
Sydney NSW 2000

Copyright © Franklin Watts 2002

ISBN: 0 7496 6238 7
Dewey Classification 306.874'3
A CIP record for this book is available from the British Library.

Printed in Malaysia

Interview on pages 12-17 by Helen Elliott, all other interviews by
Suzie Hayman

Series editor: Sarah Peutrill
Art director: Jonathan Hair
Design: Steve Prosser
Consultant: Helen Brookes, Royton and Brompton School, Oldham

Photographs: Laurence Cendrowicz, apart from:
Matt Hammill: 12-15
Paul Baldesare/Photofusion: 5b, 33, 36, 41, 44
Gina Glover/Photofusion: 34
Danny Joint/PYMCA: 5c, 38
Ute Klaphake/Photofusion: 30
5c, 5b, 30, 34, 36, 38, 41, and 44 posed by models
Every attempt has been made to clear copyright. Should
there be any inadvertent omission please apply to the
publisher for rectification.

With grateful thanks to our interviewees. Also thanks to Jenny
Glen at the Coram Parents Centre, Dionne Jude at Southwark
Council and Jenny Mcleish at the Maternity Alliance.

Contents

Introduction

Why is teenage pregnancy such a talked-about issue?

Teenage pregnancy statistics and debate are on the agenda in almost every country in the developed world. This is because, statistically, teenage mothers are less likely to finish their education and more likely to live in poverty and to rely on state benefits. In addition, the children of teenage mothers are more likely to have a low birth weight and experience health and developmental problems. Teenage pregnancy, apart from the emotional price, costs society more than adult pregnancy in lost tax revenues, public assistance and child healthcare.

Where is teenage pregnancy a problem?

In Europe, the UK has the highest teenage pregnancy rate with around 28 per 1,000 women aged 15-19 giving birth each year. Other countries in Europe have reduced their rates of teenage pregnancy over the last 20 years. For example:

◆ In the Netherlands, sex education begins in pre-school and is integrated into all levels and subjects of schooling. The country boasts one of the lowest teen birth rates in the world – 6.9 per 1,000 women aged 15-19. Likewise, their teenage abortion rate is very low, as is its overall AIDS case rate.

◆ In Germany, where sex education is comprehensive and targeted to meet the reading and developmental needs of students, the teenage birth rate is only 13 per 1,000 women.

In Australia (24 births per 1,000 women) and particularly in the USA (57 births per 1,000 women), as in the UK, it's a big issue. Could programmes similar to those in the Netherlands and Germany help in these countries?

Whose responsibility is sex education?

Some people believe that the responsibility lies with governments. They say that, nationally, there should be a clear and consistent message to teenagers about the real impact of pregnancy and parenthood and that everyone should be well educated about sex and relationships. Others think it should be left to parents to provide sex education, since sex is a personal issue. Attitudes to sex education can vary widely between people of different religions, cultures and social backgrounds.

What is it like to be a young parent?

Whatever age you are, being a parent costs - in time, effort, emotion and money. However, as you'll see from the young people here, becoming pregnant as a teenager doesn't have to ruin your life - if you have good information and support. But it is a very tough way of life. Young mothers rarely choose to raise children alone, but that's what often happens. They may end up broke, on benefits and with little or no social life. However, that's not the only story - most young mums are happy with their babies and make good mothers. Some do support themselves, live in their own home and stay with young men who do their share of the parenting.

Being a teenage father isn't easy either. As soon as the father becomes an adult with an income of his own he has to pay towards the child. And if the father has no contact, he will miss out on the benefits of having a child.

If you have never had sex:

◆ Don't worry, you are quite normal! The average age for first-time sex is 17. Many people wait longer. There's no need to rush into it.
◆ Remember, you don't have to be having sex to have a relationship. If you do want to take it further, make sure you are both well informed (see below).

If you are having sex:

◆ Take a moment to consider your experiences. Are you happy with your relationship(s)?
◆ Everyone, old or young, needs confidence and information about sex and relationships so that pregnancy isn't something that happens because of ignorance – either of how to prevent it or of what it may mean. So get informed! You can look at the websites listed on page 46 or, better still, make an appointment at your local pregnancy advisory service – it doesn't matter how old you are.
◆ Are you using contraception? If so, does it protect you against sexually transmitted infections (STIs)? For example if you are only using the pill, you will not be protected. Are you sure you are using your chosen contraception correctly? If you are a man using condoms, for example, there's nothing to stop you practising putting them on when you are alone! If you are using the pill – have you read all the instructions? Do you know when it might not work?

If you or your girlfriend is pregnant:

◆ If you can, try to talk to your partner and your parents.
◆ You have three options – keeping the baby, adoption or abortion. Read the interviews in this book, visit your local pregnancy advisory service and look at some of the websites listed on page 46 to find out more.
◆ Think about what you could be giving up, and also gaining.

It Happened to Nicola

Nicola, 17, became pregnant and gave birth to her daughter, Leonnie, at 15. At first it was a shock but she came to enjoy her pregnancy and now loves being a mother. Leonnie's father didn't want anything to do with the baby and was scared that his parents would find out.

Q When did you realise you were pregnant?

A When I was about five months pregnant. I was quite big, but up to then I didn't get any symptoms. I didn't have cravings, my body didn't feel funny, it just felt like normal. I didn't think I could be pregnant because I did have little slight shows of my period... I found it hard to believe that I was pregnant and I was scared to tell my mum. My friends were the first ones I told.

Q How did you feel?

A I felt strange. I was going to be a mother. I was

just dreaming. Shocked. But I knew from the first I'd never give up my child. Even if I'd known earlier, I'd never give up my child or have an abortion.

Q You kept your pregnancy hidden from your mum at first. Why?

A My mum was the type of person that I could talk to, but I was just so shocked.

Q How did you keep it hidden?

A I was always out. I'd come in, go to sleep and go out early again in the morning. And my mum was working at the time so she didn't really notice. When I did sit down with her I'd have a pillow in front of my belly. I was into sports at the time - like playing football, trampolining and going swimming. I was wearing baggy stuff as well to hide it. She didn't know.

Q How did you eventually tell your mum?

A I was so scared of telling her. I decided to set up an appointment for her to

Factfile - Teenage Birth Rates

Teenage birth rates, per 1,000 females aged 15-19:

◆ USA – 57
◆ New Zealand – 34
◆ UK – 28
◆ Australia – 24
◆ Germany – 13
◆ France – 10
◆ Italy – 7
◆ Netherlands – 6.9
◆ Japan – 4

come into school. My head of year was there and my tutor. We were all in the office together and I told them. I said, 'I've got some good news and some bad news'. The good news was that I was having a baby, and the bad news was that I was having a baby! It's both the same, really. My mum thought it was April Fools. Eventually she said, 'OK, you're pregnant and all we can do is what's best for the baby.'

Q What about the father?

A He didn't know until later. I didn't feel like telling him. I was scared. I was scared that he would go off. I'd known him about four months. He's a year older than me. When I eventually told him he said that he was not ready to have a child and was scared that his parents would find out. He felt like he might be letting his parents down.

" ... he said that he was not ready to have a child and was scared that his parents would find out. "

7

> **"It was a shock, but I felt happy because, I don't know, it felt like I was learning something."**

Q Do they know now?

A His parents still don't know. I'm trying to get hold of them, actually, to tell them. I don't want them to think that I'm going behind their back. I just want them to feel welcome to come and see her at any time.

Q Has the father's attitude changed?

A No he has not been a support at all. He doesn't see her - he's missing out.

Q How did you feel when you realised you were pregnant?

A I started to get quite used to it, actually. It was a shock, but I felt happy because, I don't know, it feel like I was learning something. I felt happy. I was looking forward to it. I liked the way my belly was growing. I had to read a lot of stuff and I liked finding out information. It was a good experience. Every day I was looking up something. I didn't go to [antenatal] classes but when it got to the time I knew how to do the breathing.

Q What happened at the birth?

A My mum helped me all the way through it. She told me what would happen and what I was going to go through. She told me what to expect and how to do the breathing. The staff at the hospital thought I was very good. My labour actually lasted just one hour. I did it naturally, without any drugs. It is painful though, very painful. But it's a nice experience.

It's a Fact that...

In the UK among, 16-24 year olds, 15% of men and 36% of women felt they had their first sexual intercourse too early. The younger they had been, the more likely they were to regret it.

Q Did you have any sex education at school?

A Yes, our teacher showed us how to put a condom on. But we had that after I found out I was pregnant. A bit late! I didn't like school, I used to bunk off a lot.

Q When you had the baby was the school helpful?

A My school were quite helpful. They helped me with a home tutor, keeping up to date with my exams.

" ... our teacher showed us how to put a condom on. But we had that after I found out I was pregnant. A bit late!"

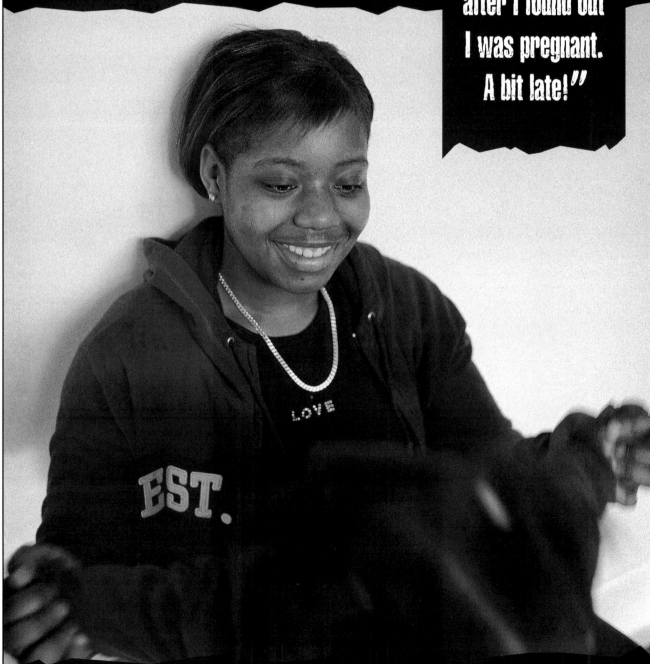

It's a Fact that...

In Australia, 54% believe parenthood would improve their relationship with their partner.

Q Now you are at college - are you more interested in education than you were at school?

A Yes, because in school I was too much with my friends. I used to hang out with my group. I found it hard to study in a big class with people talking and stuff. That's why I think the small class at college is much better. I get to do a lot more as well. I start a performing arts course in September. The course is for two years and I hope to become a singer. I'm into dancing and singing at the church I go to.

Q Do you have any regrets?

A It's good that I have had Leonnie because it has changed my life. I reckon if I didn't have Leonnie I'd be doing bad stuff now. I think having her has opened my eyes more to the world. I love being a mum. There's things I want to do, study more and get involved. It's focused me and made me think of the future.

Q How do you think young parenthood makes you change?

A Having a child changes the relationship with your parents. In my case I think it made it better. I've always got on well with my mum but we used to have arguments. I was the type of person that never used to listen. I'd always do things my way. It's true when people say, 'Always listen to your parents'. I used to think, 'Ah, mum, you're talking rubbish'. But now I'm a mum I see things from the other side, I understand. ∎

Talking Points

◆ Nicola wasn't interested in education until after the pregnancy. Why do you think this changed? What else (other than becoming a parent) might have helped her?

◆ An important part of Nicola's sex education wasn't covered until after she was pregnant. However, some people believe sex education should not begin too early because it encourages children to have sex. What do you think?

◆ Look at the teen birth rates on page 7. What reasons do you think might account for the differences in the rates?

It Happened to Kylie

Kylie lives in Melbourne, Australia. When she was 16 she discovered she was pregnant. Although she was a casual worker in a city clothing store, she had been planning to return to school to begin her final year at secondary school. The father was her then boyfriend, Manoj. Their daughter, Taylah, was four and a half months old at the time of this interview. Kylie and Manoj are no longer a couple but Manoj is actively involved with Taylah.

Q How old were you and Manoj when you discovered you were pregnant?

A I was 16 and my boyfriend was 19. We'd been together for two years.

Q Did you discuss contraception when you became more serious?

A Oh, yes! I was actually on the pill. But there was one point when I got kicked out of home for three days and it didn't even cross my mind that I hadn't taken it then, although we did have sex. Really, it just didn't cross my mind at all that I could get pregnant. I went back on the pill straight away but my period didn't come! So I stopped the pill altogether and thought I'd wait. I thought everything in my body had gone haywire. I still didn't think about being pregnant. But I waited and waited and when my period still didn't come I went to the doctor's. I was so careful except for that one time of three days. I really did not think it would happen. It was a huge shock.

Q How did you react when the doctor said you were pregnant?

A I was so shocked. Manoj came with me - he was more shocked than I was. I had both the urine test and the blood test and the lady came up to me and she was smiling, so I thought that I wasn't pregnant! And she said congratulations!

Factfile - The Pill

The pill is one of the most popular forms of birth control and very effective if taken as prescribed. There are lots of different types of pill. The two main forms are 'combined hormones' and 'progestogen-only'. Combined pills work by preventing a woman's eggs from coming to full maturity and being released from her ovaries. The progestogen-only pill works by helping the body prevent the meeting of egg and sperm and by discouraging an egg from implanting.

The most common type of pills come in a packet with 21 tablets, one to be taken daily. After taking the last one, the woman has seven days where she doesn't take a pill, and usually she has a light period (called a withdrawal bleed).

If you are on the pill, you have to remember to take it as instructed, or it may not work. It is also important to remember that sickness and diarrhoea can stop the pill from being effective. There are also some other tablets and medicines (for example, antibiotics) that can stop the pill working properly. If you only use the pill you won't be protected against sexually transmitted infections – you need to use a condom to be sure of that. See 'emergency contraception' on page 47.

Q How did your mother react when you told her?

A I didn't tell my mother. Manoj told his parents early - I could have killed him. He told them, and his mother called my mother and told her... later she came up to my room and said Manoj's mother had just called. I started crying, so she knew.

Q Did you and Manoj discuss termination?

A He did. I didn't. It's not something I'd do.

Q You're Catholic, so is it on religious grounds?

A Well, that's part of it but not all. It's more about who I am. It's not something I'd do. Ever. I did this, so I have to take the consequences. Well, not consequences, she's great - most of the time. There are times when it's very hard.

13

are. They have a group called a young mothers' clinic, which they hold every Monday evening. It's for people under 21 who are pregnant. It's especially run for young mothers to help them out. We get counselling, see a midwife, a nurse - all while you are pregnant and after.

Q What about adoption? Did that ever occur to you?

A Yes, it crossed my mind but not for long enough for me to really think about it. I wouldn't be able to do that. You carry a baby for the whole nine months, what's the point? It's really a bond thing. And even if I had chosen adoption I know that after I'd had her I wouldn't have been able to give her up. I would have always kept her.

Q Has Manoj been supportive?

A When I was pregnant he wasn't supportive, not at all. Now he's so much better. He did come to my labour which surprised me, really surprised me. I didn't know whether he was coming or not but I called him and said if he wanted he could come. So he came and he was really, really good and he's been really good since.

" [Taylah's father] comes and visits her after work and at the weekends. He still goes out every weekend but he really has settled down a lot. "

Q What was the birth like?

A It was a natural birth, no drugs although it wasn't easy. It hurts! I thought it was death pain, I thought I was dying. My ankles swelled up and I had a really bad back - I couldn't take any more pain and then she came.

Q Did you seek counselling from anyone?

A At the hospital. They were really good and still

He's settled down. He comes and visits her after work and at the weekends. He still goes out every weekend but he really has settled down a lot.

Q How has having Taylah affected your life?

A Oh, where can I start! Taylah's changed everything. My relationship with my mum has changed heaps. We're so much closer than we were. I have a great relationship with Kelly, my sister, as well. She's so good with Taylah.

Q Do you live with your family?

A Yes. It's so much easier at home. Mum helps with everything. She took a month off from her work to help me out. She is in administration at the Royal Children's Hospital and she took a month off for me! She gets to work late every morning because she's always playing with her. She's excellent with her. Having Taylah has taught me so much. Especially what I've put my mum through, so I just hope Taylah doesn't put me through anything like this.

Q What are your plans for the future?

A I really want to go back to school. I now feel very serious about that. I've changed my plans - I wanted to be a veterinarian but now I think I'd like to do nursing. I want to do something to help other people.

Q What have you had to give up?

A A lot of things, and I think about this sometimes.

> " I have a great relationship with Kelly, my sister, as well. She's so good with Taylah. "

Kylie has become closer to her family, including her sister – shown here.

15

Because I'm breast-feeding, Taylah is always with me. I can't go out with my friends as much. They do come and visit me - they've been very good like that and very supportive. I just saw a group of old school friends the other day and it was great. But there are some things it would be easier to do without her - like rushing to the bank holding her in one arm and giving money with the other. You get used to it, but it's hard. The small things are hard.

Q Describe your average day.

A Taylah wakes up at about three or four in the morning, after going to bed at around 10:30pm. I'll feed her for an hour and then she'll sleep again until around six. She'll stay awake until 10 when I give her a bath and feed her rice cereal.

It's a Fact that...

In Australia twice as many pregnant teens live in a refuge or hostel as with the father of the baby.

Then she'll have a nap and then around lunchtime I feed her again. After lunch she'll have playtime until she falls asleep at three or four. Then another feed and she's awake until the night-time. I don't have a moment to myself.

Q Would you be able to manage without your family around you?

A No. They're such a great help. Even my brother, who was sick, is such a good person with babies. He makes her laugh so much, they get along very well. On the days when I get really down and need a break I just have to see her laugh and I feel better.

Q How do you get a break?

A I just need an hour, I sometimes feel. But when I get a break I still get nervous if she isn't with me. When I go away I worry so I come back home anyway. But the early days were the hardest because you need to feed every two hours. I was just exhausted, getting no sleep at all. I don't get any sleep during the day at all now, but I get more sleep at night than I did.

Q How do you manage financially?

A Manoj gives me money every month but not as much as he should be giving. I get some money from CentreLink, Supporting Mothers' money, which I really need because she goes through a lot of nappies! I have to change her so often. It's very expensive having a baby - prams and clothes and they also grow very fast.

Q What have been the most difficult things?

A Just the responsibility of all of it. I had responsibility before, but not all that much. This all came at once and it just hits you. I knew it was

> ## "It's very expensive having a baby – prams and clothes and they also grow very fast."

all going to be hard but not as hard as it is. I sometimes think it's all too much, I can't do this. Then she'll just do something and she makes me laugh and I'm okay. I can't even remember what it was like without her now.

Q Has this changed the way you view yourself?

A Before I held Taylah I'd never held a baby in my entire life. I'd never been around them and wasn't really interested. I had to learn all those things from scratch. It brought a lot out in me that I didn't know I had. It taught me about myself, it also taught me a lot about Manoj. Taylah has tied me down, but not necessarily in a bad way. I know that if I were married to Manoj I'd have no life – I've still got heaps and heaps of things to do in life. She might

have slowed me down but she hasn't stopped me.

Q Do you think you and Manoj might end up together?

A At the moment, no – but when he's ready to commit to a family maybe things will change. I understand he's still very young and needs to do things with his friends. But maybe when he's ready I won't be around. Then he'll miss out, won't he?

Q What would you say to other girls who find they are pregnant?

A Even if your family isn't there, there's always help. Besides my family I've had

lots of help, especially the hospital and my counsellor. It's all worth it, even the hardest bits. Although I wouldn't advise anyone to do it who isn't ready to have a calm life – no drink, no knocking yourself out. This is lots of responsibility. I look at other 17 year olds and they're doing things 17 year olds do. I'll have to do other things when I'm older.

Q What does the word mother mean to you?

A Everything. It's the relationship that's closer than any other, beats sister, brother, best friend, boyfriends, girlfriends – the lot. It's the closest relationship you can ever get with anyone. ∎

Talking Points

◆ Kylie thinks getting back together with Manoj would tie her down more. Do you think having a relationship when you are young ties you down?

◆ Manoj is older than Kylie, but she still says he is very young and needs to go out with his friends. What does this show about the difference in their attitudes to being a parent? Do you think this is normal or not?

◆ How do you think Manoj might feel about being a young father?

17

It Happened to Lisa

Lisa, 17, fell pregnant at 15 and kept her pregnancy so secret that her mother didn't even know when she went into hospital to have her daughter, Summer Leigh.

Q How did you find out you were pregnant?

A I guessed because my period didn't come on. I didn't do a test until I was five months pregnant and then only because a mate made me do one. By then I was getting big. I just hid the pregnancy. My mum took me for a pregnancy test but I got my mate to give me a sample. She did ask me a couple of times, but after the pregnancy test she just believed me. She thought it was just puppy fat.

Q Why do you think she believed you?

A I've always told her everything so she just took my word for it. At school everyone was saying, 'Lisa's pregnant.' I got pulled up on it all the time - I was like, 'No, no, no, I'm not pregnant!' - it was just a nightmare. I told one person at school and then it got around. The school phoned my mum, but she said, 'If she was pregnant she would tell me'. I finally told my mum the day **after** the baby was born.

Factfile - Pregnancy Advisory Services

Pregnancy advisory services are centres, sometimes called family planning clinics, which provide a range of services including:

◆ Advice on sex and contraception
◆ Pregnancy testing
◆ Counselling
◆ Advice on or referral for abortions
◆ Referral for pregnancy services
◆ Sexually transmitted infection testing.

Pregnancy advisory services are confidential (they won't tell your parents). Addresses for local centres should be listed in your local phone directory, or you could try the addresses and websites on page 46.

Q Did you wish you had told her earlier?

A Yes, I wished I'd told her. When I saw her after, she said, 'You made me look like a complete idiot!' She was disappointed, not about the baby, but that I couldn't bring myself to tell her. But she wasn't angry or anything like that. She was just bothered about how I was. I didn't go to any antenatal [before birth] care, so I had no scans. I'd like another baby one day, not just to have a baby but to go through pregnancy and be able to express it like everyone else does. You see people walking down the street, proud to be pregnant. There was me walking down the street, shoulders hunched up and big baggy jumper on.

Q Why didn't you tell your mum if you told her everything?

A She's had a hard life and she wanted me to go to college and everything. I didn't know about benefits and the help you can get to go through college as a young mother. I thought I'd just go to hospital and give the baby up for adoption. It was only when I got to the hospital that I found out you can't until you're 18 because up to then legally the baby is the responsibility of the grandparents.

Q Did you really want to give the baby up for adoption?

A I didn't want to give her away. I just didn't want my mum to find out. It was a good job she found out. I would have regretted it.

> " The school phoned my mum, but she said, ' If she was pregnant she would tell me'. "

19

Q Who were you living with at the time?

A My mum and dad split up when I was about 10. I lived with my dad at first but now I live with my mum and my brother, he's 19. I get on very well with my brother. He found out at the same time as my mum. He was over at a friend's house and someone told him. He was shocked. But now, he loves Leigh. She does his head in sometimes but that's to be expected really.

Q What about the father?

A I'd known him about a year. He didn't know about the pregnancy until a month after she was born. He heard from a family friend who knows him as well. He came up and asked if it was true and I said yes. He apologised and he said he wanted to come to see us. He was quite good with her. He used to buy her presents. I got back together with him and then split up with him a few months later.

Q Did you want him to stay with you?

A I think our relationship had come to the end but I wanted him to stay at first for Leigh's sake. He used to help me out sometimes, but the thing is, I think he was only trying to get back with me.

Q Did you finish your school education?

A The school kept me on to do my GCSEs but let me go as soon as my exams were over. I had two exams before I had her and two after. I was breast-feeding and had to keep rushing back to feed her, it was a nightmare.

Q How did you learn about sex?

A I was bullied when I was at school so I missed a lot, including sex education. My mum taught me stuff and I knew it at quite an early age but most people don't relate sex to having babies, they just relate sex to something to do. I think that's how I probably thought as well. I was using condoms before, but obviously not that time.

Q How are you managing now?

A I think if I lived by myself I would probably have had a nervous breakdown by now. She is a very active baby - she's into everything. My mum works full-time but she helps me when I need help. She loves her and is really good with her. My brother helps quite a bit, and my best mate, Sam, comes around and takes her off my hands for a bit. But not many people help me. I go to a project, The Parents Centre, and they help. There's a nursery there and college is quite helpful. They know that I'm a young mother. Overall, I'm coping pretty well. Money is not that tight but if

> " ... most people don't relate sex to having babies, they just relate sex to something to do... that's how I probably thought as well."

I was living on my own it would be. My mum still buys the shopping and stuff like that.

Q Do you see friends?

A I wish I had more chance to go out and do stuff. I've stayed in touch with a few people from school, only the people that were really close to me. I have friends from the nursery and when I was doing an IT course I met quite a lot of mothers there.

Q So you've gone back into education?

A Yes, I've done three different courses. I've done a certificate in IT and I'm in the middle of doing intermediate business. I don't know if I want to do that now, I might leave it a couple of years until Leigh starts to calm down a bit. I've proved that you can do it. I'd thought that once I'd had a baby that was it for life, no education, no jobs. But I discovered that this wasn't true.

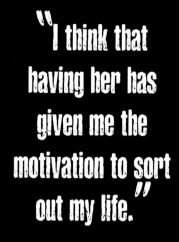

"I think that having her has given me the motivation to sort out my life."

Q How did you find out what is available?

A I went to a health centre for check-ups and they told me, and I also got a letter from Jobcentre Plus. Then my health visitor took me to the Parents Centre and Leigh got a place in the nursery. She is looked after while I study and she's been there a year now. She loves it to bits. She has lots of friends. She goes five days a week 8 till 5.30.

Q What are your eventual aims?

A At the moment, Leigh's not giving me a chance to do my work. My plan was to do the advanced course, then take a couple of years off to work and then go to university. But now I don't know whether to take a couple of years off after this course. I need to get a degree.

"It's hard not having that much money but she's worth it."

It's a Fact that...

In the UK, 20% of teenage girls and over 25% of teenage boys have had sex before the age of 16.

Q What motivates you?

A My mum told me she's now getting turned down for jobs because there's always someone with better qualifications. She's bored with her job and it's getting her down.

Q Will you stay living with your mum?

A No, we won't be at my mum's much longer because Leigh and I share a room and she'll soon need her own.

Q How do you feel about being a mum?

A I like the feeling, the feeling that she is mine. I think that having her has given me the motivation to sort out my life. She has given me a lot of options but I think a few have been taken away from me as well. It's hard not having that much money but she's worth it.

Q What would you have liked to have been different?

A More money, probably her dad still around. I wouldn't wish her away but maybe it would have

been better for her to come later rather than now.

Q If you were talking to someone else who was your age when you got pregnant, what would you say?

A Don't do it now. Wait. I wouldn't wish Leigh away for anything but it's very hard. If you're not strong-minded it's hard to cope. If you're going to have sex - be safe. Condoms are the best. ■

Talking Points

◆ Couples who have children as teenagers are less likely to stay together than couples who wait until they are older. Why do you think young people's relationships have a higher chance of ending?

◆ Lisa kept her pregnancy a secret from her mother. Why do you think she did this? What consequences might it have had? How would you feel about telling your parents you were going to become a parent?

◆ Even though Summer Leigh has a full-time place at nursery, Lisa is still finding it difficult to finish her education. Why do you think this is?

It Happened to Louise

Louise, 17, has a daughter, Latitia, aged two. Louise stayed with the father of her child for a while but had to stop seeing him when he became abusive. Louise is a good student and she is determined to become a journalist. She has already had some material published in a magazine.

Q When did you know you were pregnant?

A My mum sussed it out before me. She noticed it in my mood swings, the way I looked, the paleness of my skin. I was as skinny as ever; I was a size six. I never saw any changes so I couldn't believe in it. We went to the doctor's and I took the test, even though I didn't want to. I said, 'Why am I doing this for nothing, I'm not pregnant'. It was positive - I didn't believe it. I said to the nurse, 'No, you're wrong'. I almost fainted from the shock. I just sat down and a woman put an ice-pack on my head. Then I apologised to everyone, especially my mum. I was 15, and 14 $^1/_2$ weeks pregnant.

Q Were you using contraception?

A Yes! We'd been going out two months and that was the first time we'd slept together. It was my first time ever and we used a condom. I was ready, because I loved him. I said to myself, 'Do I want to do this?' I didn't want to get pregnant so I bought a condom and gave it to him.

Factfile - Condoms

Condoms are an excellent form of contraceptive, and are one of the easiest to get hold of and use. Both males and females can carry them. They are effective if used properly, so you always have to remember to:

◆ Check the use-by date
◆ Make sure it's on correctly (read the instructions with the packet carefully).

There are also female condoms.

He couldn't refuse because he knew that I wouldn't have sex with him if he wasn't using a condom. I thought he knew what he was doing but now I'm not so sure... I was blind because I thought he was perfect. But when he knew I was having his baby he started to do whatever he wanted, he started to change and I saw the real him.

Q Did you tell the father first?

A Yes. He guessed anyway. Then I told my dad and that took a lot of courage. I felt ashamed. I was a daddy's girl so, when I told him, I knew I'd let him down... My dad was disappointed and hurt. He didn't want me to keep the baby. He wanted me to have an abortion.

Q Did you think about abortion?

A The nurse gave me a leaflet with the options - adoption, abortion or keeping the baby. But I wouldn't be able to live and know that I killed a human being or that someone else is bringing up my child. So I thought, 'I'm going to do it. I'm going to prove to everyone that I can get through this'. All I had was determination and I got that from my mum and my dad.

Q So you made the decision before you told everyone?

A If I had made the decision to have an abortion I would have said nothing to my dad, I wouldn't even have told him I was pregnant. But because I made the decision to keep the baby, I told him.

Q Did your dad agree with your decision in the end?

A My dad was ready to follow whatever I wanted. The reason he said for me to have an abortion was because he didn't think that this would be good for my education. He knew that I

> " He couldn't refuse because he knew that I wouldn't have sex with him if he wasn't using a condom."

It's a Fact that...

Most women in the UK (well over 60%) who have unplanned births say they got pregnant because of contraceptive failure.

had always been a good student. I knew that once I had this baby I needed to get back on track - if not for me, for everyone else that I hurt.

Q What about your friends?

A I found out who my true friends were. I realised at the end of it, I never had one true friend - they were all back-stabbers. They just wanted to follow fashion, to be there because I was a girl that was well-known, well-liked and respected. When I realised that, I just lost contact with them. I just got on with my life with my mum. If it weren't for my mum, I wouldn't be where I am today and I know that. I've got a special mum. She went through a lot for me.

Q How did your sister take it?

A It really tore us apart when I got pregnant. I always loved my sister, we always had that bond where we could talk about anything. That stopped. I was grouchy because I felt stupid, ashamed. I hid in my bedroom, I never came out. She was wondering why she hadn't got a sister any more so she resented me. I know I hurt her and she didn't understand what I was going through.

Q How did your school react?

A They were shocked. I've got a friend who had a baby just before me... she wasn't allowed to go back to school because she had caused quite a bit of frustration. But they wanted me back because I was such a good student. They said it would be okay as long as I didn't brag to other girls about being pregnant. I really wanted to go back but in the end I couldn't because I was sick during my pregnancy. I could have gone back after I had Latitia as well but both of us were ill. [Louise suffered from post-natal depression].

Q Did you stay with the father?

A We were together for a year before Latitia was born, and the first five months of her life. We had a lot of ups and downs. He was violent. I still went back to him, because I wanted Latitia to be with her dad. I'm already a young parent, the least I could do was keep her father. I loved him, but he didn't want the same things in his life as I wanted.

Q How was that?

A He just wanted to lounge about at home and do nothing. But I couldn't do that. He hated the fact that I wanted to do better for myself, he got jealous. It just got worse and worse and Latitia ended up getting hurt. I wanted it to stop before she got seriously hurt.

> " I'm already a young parent, the least I could do was keep her father. "

Louise's mother has been supportive throughout.

Q How do you feel about him now?

A I want Latitia to know her father. So if he calms down a bit, his attitude changes and he's ready to do it the way I want to do it... then maybe I'll let him take her out. I do want him to see her - I wanted to do that from day one, but it's him that's missed out.

Q Have you had much support from outside the family?

A One midwife, a black lady, was nice. She deals with teenage pregnancy and she put a nice lady from 'New Deal' in touch who helped me with benefits and getting back to education.

Q What were the doctors like?

A The doctors I saw made me feel cheap, stupid and even more ashamed. They made me feel like I was making the wrong decision to keep my baby. It was like I should have an abortion because I'm a baby bringing a baby into the world. I never once had a nice doctor who said, we know it's a mistake, we know it's not planned. I'm a 15-year-old girl and I'm planning to have a baby? No, I had everything going for me and now I'm stalling my life by having a baby. I needed people to say to me we know what you've done and we know you are sorry for it. But there was no-one that did that. The doctors, they were mean. Even the nurses weren't helpful.

Q How does it feel to be a mum at your age?

A I love her, she is really important to me - she is my life. I'm not going to say that

haven't been but I have an appointment. The doctor said I've still got anger inside me. It's hard knowing that I was tricked by this boy who I loved with all my heart, and said he was going to be there for us all. He doesn't care about her the way I do. He might love her. But he doesn't show that he loves her. He's out doing whatever he's doing and I'm in with the baby.

Q What would you like to be different?

A There's been advantages from having my daughter. I've become much more mature. I know what I want and I've become even more determined to get to where I want to be. I've got to do it for her as well as me. Before, I was lazy, I couldn't be bothered but now I will do what I've got to do. I can't really say I wish I'd never had her because I'm glad I've got her.

Q What about your plans for the future?

A I want to be a journalist. I'm going to college and I want to go on to university.

> **" I saw my sister having fun, going out, doing what she wanted to do. I've got a baby who needs me constantly 24-7 – I never get a break. "**

I'm the perfect mum and have the perfect feelings. I have resented her at times. When she was four months old, there was just a week or two when I just didn't want to be at home, I didn't want to see her. I saw my sister having fun, going out, doing what she wanted to do. I've got a baby who needs me constantly 24-7 - I never get a break. She was four months old and I still had post-natal depression.

Q Have you had any support for the depression?

A My doctor told me to go for counselling. I still

Q What would your message to other young people be?

A Try your hardest not to get pregnant. That's the first thing. I've got a mother and a father who love me and will do anything for me. Not everyone is that lucky. I know I wouldn't have been able to handle it on my own and that's the truth. Now I wish I'd waited. If you meet a boy (or a girl) and they seem perfect in every way, let the relationship go further before you take that step of actually having sex - get to know them. You don't need to rush things and have sex and have babies, you just need to take your time. If you're both in love it will eventually come. Be patient! ∎

Talking Point

◆ A report on teenage pregnancy outlined three reasons why UK teenagers have such high rates of pregnancy – what do you think of their ideas?

1. **Low expectations.** In the developed world, teenage pregnancy is more common among young people who have been disadvantaged in childhood and have poor expectations of education or the job market. One reason why the UK has such high teenage pregnancy rates is that there are more young people who see no prospect of a job and fear they will end up on benefit one way or the other. Put simply, they see no reason not to get pregnant.

2. **Ignorance.** Young people lack accurate knowledge about contraception, STIs, what to expect in relationships and what it means to be a parent. Only around 50% of under 16s and 65% of 16-19s use contraception when they start to have sex, compared with around 80% in the Netherlands, Denmark and the USA. The reality of bringing up a child, often alone and usually on a low income, is not being brought home to teenagers and they are often quite unprepared for it. They do not know how easy it is to get pregnant and how hard it is to be a parent.

3. **Mixed messages.** As one teenager put it, 'It sometimes seems as if sex is compulsory but contraception is illegal'. One part of the adult world bombards teenagers with sexually explicit messages that seem to show that sexual activity is the norm. Another part, including many parents and most public institutions, is at best embarrassed and at worst silent, hoping that if sex isn't talked about, it won't happen. The result is not less sex, but less protected sex.

Source: Social Exclusion Unit

It Happened to Charlotte*

Charlotte, 18, had an abortion two years ago. She is now at university studying for a degree in English Literature.
*Not her real name.

Q When did you know you were pregnant?

A My boyfriend and I had been sleeping together for about six months. We had been taking precautions, but one night at a party we just got carried away. I was worried, of course, but I thought it would be okay. Some people try for ages to get pregnant, we couldn't be so unlucky after one time without protection. A few weeks later, I missed a period and I took a pregnancy test. It was positive.

Q What method of birth control had you been using before?

A We'd been using condoms. Simon, my boyfriend, was 18 and he wasn't embarrassed about buying them. Having an older boyfriend made me feel more confident that things would be okay.

Q Was he the first person you'd had sex with?

A Yes, we started going out just after I turned 16 and started sleeping together a few months later. We were in love and I was really happy.

Factfile - Abortion

An abortion can be carried out as soon as a woman knows she is pregnant and she is sure she does not want the pregnancy to continue. Very early abortions can therefore take place soon after a woman has missed her period.

Abortions are usually carried out within the first 12 weeks of the pregnancy (counting from the first day of the woman's last period); but in some cases they can be done up to 24 weeks (but this is rare). An abortion will only be agreed after 24 weeks if the woman's life is in danger or there is something wrong with the foetus (the developing baby).

Abortions have to be performed by a qualified doctor in a hospital or approved clinic. In the UK, the consent of two doctors is required. A doctor can refuse to consent to an abortion if she or he objects on moral grounds, but then they should refer the woman to another doctor who can give advice.

At the appointment, women see a doctor for an initial consultation. They can also choose to speak to a counsellor if they wish.

Up to 12 weeks an abortion can usually be carried out under local anaesthetic (the woman does not have to be put to sleep) and is a very simple and quick operation. If the pregnancy is between 12 and 24 weeks an abortion is more complicated and takes longer to perform.

There is very little risk associated with abortion, especially when performed early in pregnancy.

Q How did you feel when you found you were pregnant?

A I was numb. Luckily, I'd just finished my GCSEs, so I couldn't muck them up. I was expecting good grades and I was planning to do A-levels and hopefully eventually go to university. Having a baby was just not something I could consider.

Q Who did you tell first? How far along were you when you told them?

A I told my boyfriend straight away. He is two years older than me, but he was really shocked. I don't think he knew what to say. I tried to discuss it with him but he just said, 'It's up to you'. He didn't give me a hug, or try to comfort me, he just felt distant. I felt very alone then. It felt like he was wiping his hands of making a decision. But he never said he'd support me if I had the baby really, although maybe he would have. I thought at 18 he was very grown-up, but now I think he was very young. Too young to help me really.

Q When you fell pregnant, who were you living with?

A I was living my mum, dad and sister. My mum and I are very close and she saw that I was distressed about something. I think she thought I was worried about my exam results! I told her in the end, after about a week.

Q How did she react?

A She was great actually, I suppose that surprised me. I thought she'd be angry, but she was supportive. She didn't try to push me into any particular choice. She didn't want my dad to know, though, so we didn't tell him or my sister.

Q Did you think about using emergency contraception?

A I'd heard of it, but I wasn't sure how to get it. I was sure I couldn't be pregnant, though, so I didn't really think about it. When I realised my periods hadn't started it was too late.

Q Where did you learn about sex?

A Magazines mostly, I think. My parents tried to talk to me about it one time, but it was too embarrassing! I didn't want to talk about it with them. I had sex education at school and they explained that you could get pregnant after one time without protection, of course, but still I didn't think it would happen to me.

Q Did you think about going through with the pregnancy rather than having an abortion?

A My mum and I talked about all my options, but I think abortion was always the best way for me. I was looking forward to doing my A-levels and hoped to go to university. I couldn't see how I could have a baby and do all this.

Q What about adoption?

A My mum and I talked about that. I read some stuff on the Internet about it but it would still have meant months out of my life, which would have affected

It's a Fact that...

Young people who say friends and the media are their main source of information about sex have their first sexual intercourse younger than people who say school sex education is their main source.

Pro-life campaigners want abortion to be illegal.

my study. I was also worried that when I had the baby, I wouldn't want to give it up. Then I'd be thinking about it for the rest of my life; where was the baby, how was it? I couldn't deal with that thought.

Q What did you feel after the abortion?

A I never thought of it as a baby. I didn't think I was killing a baby and I still don't. I had the abortion in the really early stages - for me it had not become a baby. It was all over really quickly. It only took a few hours. I was scared but my mum came

with me. When it was over I just felt relief. I didn't feel happy, who would? But I was relieved. In the hospital I saw all kinds of other women - I'd thought they'd all be like me, teenagers, but there were all sorts of women there. For a few weeks after, though, I felt depressed, I kept wondering if I'd done the right thing - it was an awful time.

Q Did you tell anyone else?

A Not at the time. My mum and boyfriend knew, of course, but I didn't want anyone else to know. I just

wanted to get on with my life. Since I've been at university a really good friend told me she had an abortion, so I told her about mine. It was good to talk to someone who had the same experience. I didn't think the

> " I never thought of it as a baby. I didn't think I was killing a baby and I still don't. "

abortion had affected me so much, but when we talked about it, I found that I had a lot more feelings about it - some of guilt, but also wondering what my life would have been if I'd had the baby.

Q How did your boyfriend feel about it?

A He was relieved too, I think. He wanted to talk about it, but I wanted to just get on with my life. We broke up soon after. I thought I'd be unhappy about that, we were in love and everything but in the end it just seemed easier to break up.

It's a Fact that...

In the UK, between 30 and 40% of women have an abortion at some point in their lives.

In the UK, abortion has been legal for over 30 years, and only 8% of the population think that it should not be.

Q How do you feel about sex now?

A I would never take a risk like that again. I'm on the pill now, although I'm not seeing anyone. I would still insist

they use a condom as well - to be really safe.

Q What's your life like now?

A I'm really happy at university, I've made lots

of friends and am enjoying my life. I have avoided relationships but I'm beginning to feel more hopeful about that. I'm so grateful that the abortion gave me the choice to do all this. I mean, I know some people have children and carry on with their education, but I know how hard that must be. It wasn't something I could have done. I have freedom to do what I want to do. I couldn't have done that if I'd had a baby.

Q How do you feel about the abortion now?

A I really wish it hadn't happened. It was the worst experience of my life, but I don't think it was the wrong decision. I think about it a lot. I couldn't provide the life I would want to give my children. I had a happy, stable upbringing - I want the same for my children.

Q How do you see your future?

A I'm going to work hard and get a good degree. Who knows after that, I'd quite like to travel - see the world. One day I'd like to get married and settle down and have children. I want

to choose the right time, though. I want to do it on my terms.

Q What would you say to a friend who was considering having an abortion?

A I don't think any two situations are the same. Everyone has to make their own decisions - but I think it's always best to get as much information about a situation as you can - by talking to people or whatever. It's always easier when you've got someone to talk to. ■

> "I really wish it hadn't happened. It was the worst experience of my life, but I don't think it was the wrong decision."

Talking Points

◆ Some people who are 'pro-life' are against abortion, as they believe it involves killing a human being. Others are 'pro-choice' – they believe the woman has the right to choose to have the baby or abort the foetus. What do you think?

◆ Charlotte now thinks her ex-boyfriend is younger emotionally than she originally thought. Why do you think this is? What do you think of his attitude?

◆ Charlotte's decision was hard to make but she clearly feels she did the right thing. How do you think you would feel if it were you?

It Happened to Tim

Tim is 16. Six months ago, his girlfriend told him she was pregnant.

Q When did you know your girlfriend was pregnant?

A I hadn't seen her for a few days because she bunked off school. I thought she was sick, bunking off wasn't her style. I rang her and she had her phone turned off, or didn't answer, so I went round and she told me.

Q How did you feel when you found she was pregnant?

A I nearly messed my pants, if you want to know! After, I thought, 'Oh, I can start a baby!' but it didn't make me proud like I thought it would. It made me feel stupid that I'd got myself into this. We'd been together about six months and having sex about three. I really liked her, but being a dad wasn't in my plans.

Q What did you do?

A I said I'd be there for her - what else can you say? But I wasn't sure what

Factfile - Teenage Fathers

> " We'd been together about six months and having sex about three. I really liked her but being a dad wasn't in my plans. "

Factfile - Teenage Fathers

Teenage boys who father a child may find that they face a different set of problems to the girl involved, for example:

◆ The girl may ask what he thinks but he has no rights in the decision whether to keep, abort or have the child adopted.

◆ If the mother decides to have the child, many teenage fathers find it difficult to stay in touch even when they want to be involved. They may be excluded from their child's upbringing by the girl's family.

◆ The fact that he has a child won't be taken into account if a teenage father applies for housing. So it may be unsuitable and he won't be able to have his child to stay.

◆ Even if he had no say in the outcome of the pregnancy and no contact, a father is responsible for the upkeep of his child. This is true whatever his age when the child was conceived although he may not have to start paying until he is 18. In the UK the Child Support Agency may require him to contribute up to a quarter of his income.

I meant or anything. I was so scared at what my parents would say. I'm going to university, so is she - how were we going to do it with a baby?

Q Were you using birth control?

A We used condoms but not that time. I'd say they spoiled it but that's not the truth. This one time, I went off when I was just putting it on, and another time I put it on the wrong way and it tore. So every time I used one, I'd be thinking, 'Am I going to look like an idiot this time?' so I'd make excuses not to use them. Stupid, stupid, stupid!

Q Did you have sex education at school?

A We were going to but some parent complained about it. So all we did was 'Reproduction' - of rabbits, and a little on contraception, but not much. A cousin of mine, he goes to a school that does it properly. He says they have all sorts of discussions and get to talk about why you do it and how you react - relationships, stuff like that. We both had sex with our girlfriends, but he didn't get his pregnant.

" I was relieved, I won't lie, but I did feel as if it wasn't fair, I didn't have a say and she never asked me, nor did anyone else. "

He says I should have practised with a condom on my own and then I wouldn't have made such a mess of it. I hadn't thought of that.

Q Did you talk about what you were going to do?

A Not really. I sort of said something about abortion and adoption but I didn't know what I was talking about and neither did she, really. I didn't see her for a few days and then she just rang me up and said she was having an abortion, no arguments - nothing to do with me. I was relieved, I won't lie, but I did feel as if it wasn't fair, I didn't have a say and she never asked me, nor did anyone else.

Q What did your parents say?

A I didn't tell them, until after the abortion. I didn't

It's a Fact that...

Confidential services in secondary schools in the United States which include contraceptives and sexual health advice have neither encouraged nor discouraged young people to have sex. But they have increased the contraceptive use among those that do.

In Australia, 90% of all teenage pregnancies are unplanned and about half of these end in abortion.

---

want them going round seeing her and interfering. My mum cried and said it was her fault for not saying something about birth control. My dad was quiet. He never told me off, he just went sad. I didn't think till later. I've got a brother and a sister, both older, both married. But I was the first one to start a baby. Their first grandchild. It was my brother said this to me, I didn't think about it. It made me feel, well, bad. Not because of the abortion, it was the only way and I can't blame her or me for it. But for starting something I couldn't finish, without thinking.

Q Are you still seeing her?

A No. I wanted to go with her to the hospital and we were on the phone and she kept saying no. I rang one time and her mum snatched it out of her hand and screamed down the phone at me, saying she'd get the police on me if I tried to see her again. I didn't ring her again and when she came back to school, we didn't talk. She cut me dead. That really hurt.

Q Did you tell any of your friends?

A Just my cousin who is a good mate. I can't tell any of my other friends. I think some of them would think it was big, getting a girl pregnant. Or some of them would be on her side and think I'd taken advantage and gang up on me. Either way, it's not the way it was. There were faults on both sides, we both should have been more careful. And she was the one who dropped me, not the other way. I put my hands up to being an idiot and not thinking, and I'll do better next time. I mean, next time I have a girlfriend I'm going to be so careful, really. It's made me and my parents talk a lot more. That's good.

> "...when she came back to school, we didn't talk. She cut me dead. That really hurt."

Q Has anything changed now?

A All my family have wanted to talk about it. In fact, the worst thing was that my parents blame themselves for not telling me more - so now it's all sex education books and family discussions at our house - BORING!! My sister was really nice, it's made us close which we've never been before. My brother said he felt bad about not being there for me - there's ten years between us, eight between me and my sister. They were always brother and sister with me sort of left out. Now they make a bit more effort to talk to me, which felt a bit odd at first but now it's good.

Q What would you have liked to have been different?

A Better sex education at school - not just facts. I knew most of the facts, I'd like to have talked about what you feel and how you act. My cousin is a year older than me and he had sex first the same time as I did. He

It's a Fact that...

In any one year, if you are having heterosexual sex and do not use contraception you have a 90% chance of conceiving.

and his girlfriend are really tight and still together. I might have done better if my school hadn't been so uptight. Or it would have been better if we'd talked about it together, not have her go off on her own. I was scared but I didn't want her to face it on her own. I think that's why her parents thought I was the one to blame, because she thought she was on her own.

Q What have you learned?

A Well, I can't put the blame everywhere but on me. I was an idiot. What have I learned? To use a condom properly, every time! And think about it - no use risking it unless it's really worth it. I had a chance of a jump at a party a few weeks ago. I turned it

down. It could have been a few minutes' gain for a lifetime of pain. Never again.

" I was scared but I didn't want her to face it on her own. I think that's why her parents thought I was the one to blame, because she thought she was on her own."

40

Tim is relieved that he doesn't have the responsibility of being a father, like this teenage boy.

Q How do you feel about yourself and your future?

A You could think it's a lucky escape but it wasn't. That was my first real girlfriend and I ended up feeling bad about myself and her hating me. I've only got a few more months in this school and then it's sixth-form college. I've made sure we'll be in different ones. I want a fresh start. Then I'm going to university and I'm going to make something of myself. I have to, or I'm going to feel bad about myself forever. ■

Talking Points

◆ Tim feels that the sex education he had at school let him down. Do you think he is right? Should schools be the main source of information about sex?

◆ As in the case of a lot of unwanted pregnancies, the father was not given a say in what happened. Is this fair? Should he have been involved more?

◆ Why do you think some people think, 'It won't happen to me' when they have sex without contraception? What can be done to change this?

It Happened to Irina

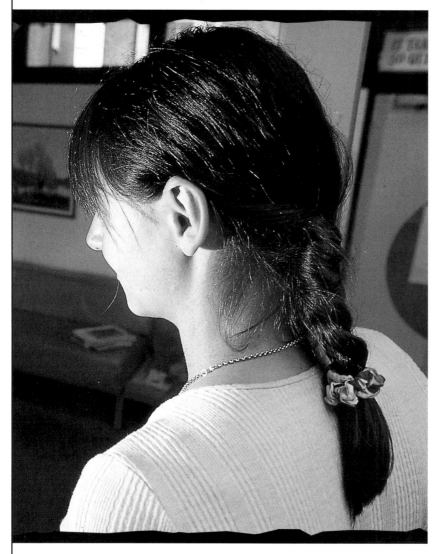

Irina is an asylum seeker, originally from Kosovo, but now living in the UK. She is 18 and has a two-year-old son. She is a volunteer interpreter for an asylum-seekers centre, in Oxford. She is living with her boyfriend, who joined her after she moved to Oxford. In this interview she calls her partner her 'husband', even though they are not married – as this is how she would like others to see him.

Q How did you find out you were pregnant?

A I was 16 when I arrived in this country. I left Kosovo because of all the bad things that were happening there. I went to the doctors' and asked them to check me out. They told me I was pregnant. I felt terrible. I cried for about three months. I thought, 'What shall I do?' I was young, and I thought I don't want this now. I need to go to college and study first.

Q Did you know you might get pregnant?

A I didn't know anything about being pregnant. I didn't plan it, it was accidental that I got pregnant. I didn't know about contraception - in my country, they didn't explain anything to me. We don't have sex education. My parents didn't know I was in love with someone, they told me nothing.

Q What about the father?

A My parents didn't speak with me for eight months because his religion is not the same as mine. My parents didn't want me to get married with him and they still don't. I was not living with him then, we stayed separated for a long time. I didn't feel very happy, I felt very, very bad. I wondered where I was going to be with my baby. I'm still not married but my baby's father is with me now. One day I think we will get married.

Q Did he want to have the baby?

A My husband said to me, 'We should have this baby, maybe this baby is lucky'. But it was a really hard time. I had no-one to talk about it with, no-one came to me to say don't worry, these things happen. I love my parents a lot and I really miss them. They were really worried about me, how I got pregnant, how I will manage. I love my son, but it's really hard for me, and I'm very tired.

> **" I love my son, but it's really hard for me, and I'm very tired."**

It's a Fact that...

Babies born to teenage mothers are more likely to have low birth weights, childhood health problems and accidents and be admitted to hospital.

Q What was your pregnancy like?

A When I was pregnant I went to the doctor and I was anaemic because I couldn't eat properly. I didn't have a kitchen and just had to buy things like kebabs, fish and chips. It was very expensive.

Q Did you have any money?

A Mainly vouchers [asylum seekers are sometimes given food vouchers instead of money]. The vouchers were a problem because I was pregnant and my body needed fruit, and also the vouchers were just for one supermarket, which is very expensive. If I took shampoo or something to wash with... they said to me you are not allowed this. You are only allowed to buy food. Other people go and buy normally, but when they see vouchers they feel oh, a refugee, like this, a bad reaction.

Q Where did you live?

A Social services put me in a house and anyone could be there. I couldn't have a shower - every moment the boys come in the bathroom. I was pregnant, and I needed to go in there often. In the hostel we had to share a room with one other person. It's really difficult to be with a person who you don't know. I couldn't stay there, I told them, 'I'm pregnant, I want more help,' but they didn't listen. Then they said, 'We will put you in a house that is very good, a really nice place'.

Q What was this hostel like?

A When I went there it was the same - a lot of boys there, I was the only girl. Every day I started going to social services, but they said, 'The hostel is very good, why are you coming again?' In the hotel there was no kitchen and the bathroom was really very dirty. They gave me £25 in vouchers and breakfast in the hotel, which was not nice food at all. I stayed in the hotel for six months. There were insects there. When you are pregnant you need more help, more care, more everything. After that my friends arrived in Oxford and they said to me, 'You can come here'.

Q Did moving out of London help?

A It was a complete change when I came to Oxford. I didn't have any friends in London, I was really worried. I need friends to talk to. I was very lonely. Now I make friends from my work, from my college. It's nice when you meet people, speak to people, share everything with them. If you don't have anyone to speak to, it's very sad, especially when you are young, because you have a lot of problems that you have to share with someone, and the best is friends.

Some pregnant teenagers find it a difficult time, as Irina did.

Q Where did you live at first?

A When I came to Oxford I stayed for three months in a house sharing with other people. For three months I cooked for eight people there, and washed, ironed everything

" If you don't have anyone to speak to it's very sad... "

44

It's a Fact that...

Daughters of teenage parents have a higher chance of becoming teenage mothers themselves.

- it was very, very hard. No one looked after me. But after I had the baby they [social services] moved me to a house. It was very nice. Every day I think, Oh! I have a house, I can't believe it.

Q You are studying now?

A I studied for one year, and now I'm doing a one-year International Study Programme, which prepares you to go to university. I need to study, I love studying. My husband is also at college because we are both just 18.

Q Who looks after the baby?

A My husband looks after the baby when I'm at work. But when he has a job, or goes out, or goes to college, I have to look after him. Sometimes my friends help, but we don't know people very well, so we have to be careful. I am really busy, and very tired!

Q How is the money situation now?

A Now I'm getting money because I have a child. My son is very little. Children need a lot of things! It's quite expensive because I pay all the bills. But I have more choice.

Q How are you coping now?

A I come here [an asylum-seekers centre] and work, which I very much like. I like to help people and I know what it means to be poor, because I come from a poor background. My family was really, really poor. I want to make something for my future now, and to work hard. This is a very safe place for my son, for me, and for my husband.

Q What about your future?

A I think a lot about this... I'm in college, studying, and this year I'm going to university to study law. I work very hard to find something because I don't want to leave my parents for nothing. It's always painful to me, knowing they are far away and how they felt about the baby. Having a baby is a big thing. ■

Talking Points

◆ According to a UK-wide study, 80% of young women regret their early sexual experience. How would you persuade a friend, or what reasons would you give to your boy or girlfriend, to wait until later?

◆ Irina had no sex education at all in Kosovo. Why do you think some people/cultures prefer not to educate young people about sex?

Useful addresses and contacts

Brook
Provides youth advisory and birth control clinics for young people. Gives sexual advice, carries out pregnancy tests and offers help and support for unplanned pregnancy.

Freephone: 0800 0185 023
www.brook.org.uk

Sexwise
A free, confidential helpline for teenagers on any aspect of sex and personal relationships.

Freephone: 0800 282930.

National Council For One Parent Families
Publishes the *Lone Parent Handbook* with all the details on getting back to education and work, childcare, housing, benefits, money and legal matters.

255 Kentish Town Road
London NW5 2LX
Tel: 020 7428 5400
Freephone lone parent helpline:
0800 018 5026
www.oneparentfamilies.org.uk

Youth Access
Provides information including the location of your nearest youth advisory centre.

1-2 Taylors Yard
67 Alderbrook Road
London SW12 8AD
Tel: 020 8772 9900
www.youthaccess.org.uk

Marie Stopes
Promotes the acceptance of family planning techniques and runs health and family planning programmes.

153-157 Cleveland Street
London W1T 6QW
Tel: 020 7574 7400
www.mariestopes.org.uk

bpas
Has clinics throughout the UK offering pregnancy testing, emergency contraception, counselling and abortion care.

Austy Manor, Wootton Wawen, Henley in Arden
B95 6BX
Tel: 01564 793225
www.bpas.org

National Childbirth Trust
For information on childbirth and breast feeding.

Alexandra House
Oldham Terrace, Acton
London W3 6NH
Enquiry Line: 0870 444 8707
www.nctpregnancyandbabycare.com

Maternity Alliance
For information about rights and services.

Third Floor West,
2-6 Northburgh Street,
London EC1V 0AY
Information line: 020 7490 7638
www.maternityalliance.org.uk

Fostering Network
Information on adoption and fostering.

87 Blackfriars Road
London SE1 8HA
Tel: 020 7620 6400
www.fosteringnetwork.net

The Site
Advice on youth centres near you plus information on sex, birth control and relationships.

www.thesite.org.uk

AUSTRALIA
Pregnancy Counselling Link
Helps with concerns or queries related to unplanned or unwanted pregnancy. Includes factsheets on unplanned pregnancy, abortion and teenage pregnancy.

Level 2, Bowman House
276 Edward Street
Brisbane
Free counselling service: 1800 777 690
www.pcl.org.au

Marie Stopes International Australia
Promotes the acceptance of family planning techniques and runs health and family planning programmes.

PO Box 6308, St Kilda Road Central, Melbourne,
Victoria 8008
Tel: (03) 9525 2411
www.mariestopes.org.au

Glossary

abortion When a pregnancy ends and does not result in the birth of a child. Abortions can be spontaneous (or natural), when they may also be called miscarriages. They can also be medically induced - called termination of pregnancy. See page 31.

adoption When a child is given to people who are not his or her birth parents for them to raise. Adoptive parents are always carefully screened for their suitability as parents.

anaemic When blood has a low level of red cells, leading to pale colouring and tiredness.

antenatal class A class for pregnant women (and their partners) that explains how to keep healthy during pregnancy and what happens and what to do during birth and after.

conception The moment when a sperm fertilises an egg.

condom A tube of very thin rubber, which is closed at one end, that a man puts over his penis before sexual intercourse. It is used as a contraceptive and also to stop sexual infections. See page 25.

consent, age of The age at which people are legally allowed to say yes to sex. The age varies between countries. In the UK and Australia it is 16.

contraceptive Something that stops a woman getting pregnant. The most popular methods are the pill and condoms (see pages 13 and 25), but other methods such as injectable contraception are available. Doctors and local family planning centres give advice as to which form of contraceptive is best for each person.

emergency contraception There are two types of emergency contraception - pills and IUDs. Pills can be taken up to 72 hours (three days) from the time of unprotected sex. They provide special, stronger dose of contraceptive hormones, given for a very short time (usually two doses of two pills, 12 hours apart). The pills may delay the release of an egg from the ovary, or they may change the womb lining slightly for a short time, so it's very difficult for a fertilised egg to implant in the womb lining. This means it cannot develop into a pregnancy. An IUD works in a similar way but can be inserted up to 96 hours or 4 days after unprotected sex. Emergency contraception is not a form of abortion because it prevents a pregnancy occurring. The sooner it is used the more effective it is.

family planning A general term to describe deciding how many children you want to have. Also refers to the methods you can use which are also called contraception and birth control.

foetus An unborn baby, more than eight weeks after conception.

natural birth When a mother gives birth without taking drugs to help with the pain.

period The common term for the time when a woman is menstruating - when the lining of her womb is discharged and she bleeds, usually for about 5-7 days. When a woman is pregnant her periods usually cease and so this is one of the signs of pregnancy.

pill, the A form of contraceptive, taken by a woman. See page 13.

precautions An informal way of talking about contraceptives.

pregnancy test A way of determining if a woman is pregnant. A test can be bought from a chemist or carried out by a doctor or family planning clinic. Pregnancy can be determined from a sample of the woman's urine or a blood test.

pro-choice Someone who is in favour of the right for a woman to choose to have an abortion if she thinks it is necessary.

pro-life Someone who believes that abortion is wrong - that the life of the unborn child should be preserved.

sexual intercourse The physical act of sex between people.

sexually transmitted infection (STI) Infections such as HIV, chlamydia and gonorrhoea, amongst others. Most STIs can be easily diagnosed and treated, but some have serious consequences. The best way to avoid them is to use condoms during sexual intercourse.

termination A medically induced abortion.

Index

Getting active!

On your own:
'It's better to leave parenthood until the parents are married and have a secure financial background.' Write a short piece explaining whether you agree or disagree with this statement.

In pairs:
Conduct a survey of young people to gain an insight into their views about teenage pregnancy. Think of five questions to ask and get as many responses as possible. Present your results in an easy-to-view format such as a chart or table.

In groups:
Put together ideas for a campaign from the government to explain safe sex to teenagers and reduce the number of teenage pregnancies. Research countries that have lower rates of teenage pregnancies – why is this? Think about the different areas of the campaign – national advertising, school education, health services etc.